MATTERS OF THE HEART

CONNIE VICTORIA VOLK

DEDICATION

This book is dedicated to

my father,

Edwin R. Ehrman,

whose one and only poem forged a path for

me to believe

I too could write, igniting sparks of life

within the hearts of others.

THE GEM

"If there is Love in your heart,

Which forms a tear in your eye,

It is truly a precious gem

Which can never be bought or sold

And reaches into eternity."

Written by

Edwin R. Ehrman

At 3:02 a.m., Nov. 17, 1984

It was written on a simple notecard.

I still have that notecard. It has become one

of my special treasures.

ACKNOWLEDGEMENTS

Writing a book is not a solitary adventure, so special thanks to the members of the Wordsmiths:

Gayle Larson Schuck

Andra Marquardt

Norma Nichols

Mel Bullinger

They were all a constant encouragement to me.

Their humor, honesty, practical knowledge and helpful suggestions created the impetus I needed to complete this book.

A special thanks to Betty Mertz for the inspiration leading to the selection, *Interchanges of a Revealing Kind.*

Also, many thanks to Mary Schmitz for her excellent job of formatting and uploading the book.

Her tidbits of wisdom and cheerful attitude refreshed me regularly along the way, and she always had a solution for all technology issues.

TABLE OF CONTENTS

PREFACE

Matters of the Heart is set against the background of life. It is to be experienced by the heart, not analyzed by the mind.

It is a book that simply cannot be tied down to either prose or poetry. The selections defy normal boundaries. So do our hearts—as they sink in sorrow, rise in joy, bow in humility or worship in adoration.

Over a period of eleven years, these selections evolved from random writings into a pattern for maneuvering through life. They bridge the gap between rejection and acceptance, despondency and joy. They flow from our past into the sunshine of a new day. They grab at the truth embedded in our hearts by the Creator Himself and pull us forward into an abundant life.

The poetry itself is designed to catch the
wind of the Spirit. Feel free to flow with it.
Let the words roll off your tongue, be picked
up by your ears and tickle your toes. Lean
into it. Enjoy the interplay of the rhythms,
the sounds and the pauses. Savor the flavor
of the words. Let the experience be fun.
Experiment with reading the selections
aloud, varying the pitch of your voice and
the speed at which you move from line to
line. Immerse yourself in your awakened
emotions. Allow them to touch your heart
and soak into your soul, making them your
very own.

Welcome to the journey.

INTRODUCTION

Explore the pathways of a heart in motion, moving…

Out of the past,

Through transitions,

Into victory,

Upward in joy,

Into rest,

Forward in revelation,

Toward glimpses of the eternal realm and, finally,

By fire, into intimacy.

Teardrops of fire

from the eyes of God

dropping

into the hearts of men...

THE PAST

"Forget the former things; do not dwell on the past. See, I am doing a new thing! Now it springs up; do you not perceive it?"

Is. 43:18 NIV

THE PAST

There she sat, with head erect, on a cold pew toward the back of the church. So stately in appearance she was, sitting next to the aisle. You couldn't miss seeing her.

She looked vaguely familiar, like I'd seen her a long time ago; but I couldn't be sure. When I bent down to ask if we had met before, I received an almost imperceptible nod. Her frame was small and frail, without the strength to move.

It was her eyes that drew my greatest attention—old, so old, with no spark of life, faded to the point of no distinct color.

This was my past?!

I had allowed this wax-like figure to influence my present and limit my future?

How foolish it all now seemed.

With one final look, I turn my back on the wax-like figure and walk out the double doors, into my future.

"...I do have one compelling focus: I forget all of the past as I fasten my heart to the future instead."

Phil. 3:13b TPT

THE BATTERY OF THE PAST

See it not?

Look towards the headwaters of your heart.

There it lays, but not at rest.

It is the old, dead battery of the past,

leaking bitter acid into your stream of life…

just as destructive as

corroding rejection,

eroding shame,

abrasive anger…

all eating away at the joy of life.

***

Allow Me to love you, says Father…

applying the Blood

to alkalize your belly

to neutralize the acid.

Be whole again, be clean

Lean towards Me.

Receive My love.

"Your old life is dead. Your new life, which is your real life—even though invisible to spectators—is with Christ in God."
Col. 3:3-4 MSG

THE STRONGHOLD

The walls rose ever so slowly,
taking place within the quiet passing of time.
Years of time.

Fashioned bit by bit from the clay of
disappointment, the blocks grew in strength
with each additional layer—the limestone of
hurt, the sand of strength-depleted, the sulfur
of frustration and the silt of hope deferred.

Tears of grief watered the blocks
while the smoldering heat of suppressed
anger baked them.

When cooled, the heavy blocks were
positioned atop one another, one by one.

I erected such a prison that it took
Your love-pierced light of truth and my
empowering decree of victory to bring it
tumbling down…in an instant.

Now, I, the prisoner, walk free of the rubble

and into the light of joy!

Psalm 81:10 TPT

ICE CREAM HEAVEN

Reluctant to get out of bed just yet and leave the heavenly presence of the King, I bask in the early morning sunshine streaming through my east window. I allow my thoughts to carry me back in time to my childhood bedroom on the second floor of the white, square farmhouse my grandfather built. That home was replete with memories, mostly happy, but also sprinkled with others I would rather shed.

"Then come with Me," Jesus said, "to the most delightful of all places—ice cream heaven. That's where all old childhood issues are melted away."

I take Him up on His offer.

How easy! How fun! Here's how it worked.

The scary face of fear at the top corner of my bedroom melted like hot chocolate, running down the corner wall and ending up on the floor as fudge. I got to stomp on it with my bare feet.

The old, confining rails of my crib turned into my favorite flavored popsicles. What fun to slurp on them, turning my cheeks into picturesque designs of orange, grape and raspberry.

When weariness overtook me, I got to lay down and relax on a comfy bed of vanilla scoops of ice cream topped with Maraschino joy cherries.

Unwanted intrusions of darkness were immediately frozen into dilly bars, dipped in the hardened chocolate coating of heaven's Dairy Queen.

Disappointments were blended into root beer floats and disappeared.

My faithful German Sheperd dog,
Sheppie, eagerly licked away my blueberry
tears of regret while colored sprinkles of
laughter filled the air.

The hard knocks of childhood soon got
crunched up into Baby Ruth flavored
blizzards.

Finally, the issues of the past are cleaned
up.

Content and happy, I slip back home in my
memories to rest in that yellow lace
curtained farm bedroom, still a child at
heart…free to laugh and love again in life's
sunshine.

A TOUCH OF GOD

Five laparoscopic incisions had been used to cut open and intrude upon the smooth skin of her left shoulder.

Now the time had come for the thick covering of blood-soaked gauze and bandages to be removed.

Long, slender fingers began their task. One hand held the adjacent skin firm and secure. The other hand began to gently pry away the edges of tape holding the huge bandage in place.

One by one by one. It seemed to be an endless procession of tape, but her fingers worked with the caress of a mother caring for her newborn infant. The soft tenderness of her heart was continually transmitted through the movements of her hands. They radiated the touch of love to a hurting, injured shoulder.

It was the gentleness of the Spirit of God flowing through human hands to heal a wounded body and soul.

THE VISIT

The Spirit of Jesus came to visit today.

He brought fresh flowers, a happy smile and a helping hand. Warm soup, muffins, candy, homemade bread and a hearty meal did accompany…also, a ride when needed, items from the store, a jar opened, a clean kitchen floor.

Don't forget the hug, text and book, the calls, cards and prayers—all were thoughts orchestrated by the One above.

Hands of service—they touched and soothed, rubbed and peeled, positioned belts, cooked and cleaned.

The body of Christ in action—that's what it was. Looking back, the coordinated effort I now can see.

Yes, the Spirit of Jesus came to visit today.

He arrived, looking just like you!

Thank you!

"For the body (of Christ) does not consist of one member but of many."

I Cor. 12:14 RSV

A COMPLETE CLEANSING

Not just in part but the whole…

not just the presentable, but also the

unpresentable

the recognizable and the unrecognizable

the fruitful along with the unfruitful

the clean and the stained

the mended with the torn

the smooth, the ragged

the healed and the wounded.

"Wash me, and I will be whiter than snow."

Psalm 51:7b NIV

OUT

Out of irritation, a pearl.

Out of obscurity, sight.

Out of poverty, riches.

Out of conflict, peace.

Out of sorrow, joy.

Out of ashes, life.

Come out. Come out. Come out!

"But I have chosen you out of the world..."

John 15:19b KJV

TRANSITIONS

"...however I do have one compelling focus: I forget all of the past as I fasten my heart to the future instead. I run straight for the divine invitation of reaching the heavenly goal and gaining the victory-prize through the anointing of Jesus."
Phil. 3:13b-14 TPT

THE LIE

The big black hole in my heart lies ripped
open,

    the lie…the enormity of it…exposed.
"I see it now, Lord. I thought You left me; I
thought You left me all alone."
Flashback:
  Back to the Garden…
   "Did God really say…?"
    Doubt
     Doubting the truth
      Believing the lie.
Flashback:
  Resurrection morning…
   The tomb is empty,
    But the big black hole is filled, filled
with light and Truth.
     It has become the garden wherein He
stands.

Now, you need to stand up.

Put on the belt of truth.

Live in the TRUTH.

"I don't believe any lies, and I don't tell any either.

The lies were exposed on the cross, and I go free, free, free."

"So if the Son sets you free, you will be free indeed."

John 8:36 ESV

THE PORTRAIT OF A HEART

I stand before a veiled portrait of my heart. It has been almost a lifetime in the making.

Now, expectation…

In a flash, the veil is dropped. My eyes are opened, and I can see.

Amazed, I stand and gaze…

Shock.

"Lord! Is this really what I'm seeing? Half a heart? One side pulsing with life, but the other side marred and scarred?"

A sight to behold…

raw, red meat, gnawed on and devoured by locusts of misperceptions, loneliness, rejection—

breathing…but only half alive

tender to the touch…offendable

lonely, forsaken…closed off, shut off
.

walls of protection…nobody in, nobody out

nothing in, nothing out,

a state of denial… "Oh, I'm good. I'm fine."

Desperation: "Jesus! How can I go on like this? With only half a heart?"

***

He comes, *lowly and riding on a donkey*. In the *fullness of time*. He knows. He sees. He understands. For He was also *rejected by men, a man of sorrows and acquainted with grief*. Misunderstood and hated by those He loved. A spear *pierced his side. Blood and water poured out*…a broken heart.

So now, He stands before me. In His hands,

half a heart.

There for the taking.

"May I join My heart with yours?"

"Yes, my Lord King."

Two hearts… now beating as

one…connected, flowing, intermingled.

And the portrait is transformed with life!

Zech. 9:9; Gal. 4:4; Is. 53:3; John 19:34

NKJV

SNOWED UNDER

What're you doing so down low…
struggling in the snow,
smothered with regret,
trying to forget?

Do you not see the sun above?
My Son melts it all with love.

Leave behind the old regrets.
You're not meant to fret.
Release to me your loss,
Leave it at the cross.

A burden, life is not meant to be.
But, rather, an adventure…
Drawing you to Me.
Be free.

SWALLOWED

Swallowed by love
Swallowed whole…

every doorway of my heart swung open to
the digestive juices of love…
eating away the acid of bitterness,
expanding the arterial walls of hard-hearted
plaque,
flushing the joints of arthritic unforgiveness,
releasing the pressured nerves of stress,
resetting the switches of glandular excess.

Swallowed by love.
Immersed in love.
Free to love.

PRIDE/HUMILITY

One sure, clean cut of the knife, one swift
pull of the pliers
and the shiny skin of the fish is removed.
　　　　　　The flesh lies exposed for all
to see.

One sure, clean cut of the façade, one swift
removal of the mask
And the shiny face of pride is removed.
The heart lies exposed for all to see.

The atmosphere of humility now allows the
once stony heart to breathe again.
It allows the humble heart to be true again—
to itself, to others.

It lives.
It moves and comes into being.

It weeps great tears of freedom.

It now can be touched.
It now can be loved.

MAKING A DIFFERENCE

(COMPANION POEMS)

REJECTION

Not a word spoken,

but an attitude conveyed, and a heart swayed

away

from innate love to guilt and self-hate.

Not a move made,

but a shock wave felt by a heart shoved

into a corner, placed upon a shelf.

Not a greeting shared,

but a cold, hard stare sending a heart into

the depths of despair.

"No chance, no hope.

No hope, no life."

Gone! Gone now…into the emptiness of

nothingness.

ACCEPTANCE

A word spoken,

and an attitude conveyed to an empty heart.

"You are noticed. You matter. You are

missed."

A move made,

and warmth felt in a heart brought

out of a corner and taken down from a shelf.

A greeting shared,

and a word of appreciation pulling

a heart back from the depths of despair.

"I'm seen. I'm loved.

There is yet hope. There is yet life."

A heart revived…to dive back in and thrive!

THE TENDRILS

The vine-like tendrils of the Spirit reach out, gently and softly feeling their way along the cracked, coarse surface of a heart…until contact is made with the appropriate "grab hold."

The tendrils of love attach.

And then begins the process of softening that heart of stone—lovingly and tenderly transforming it into a heart of flesh…one made in the image of God.

"I will take the heart of stone out of your flesh and give you a heart of flesh."
Ezek. 36:26 NKJV

THE MAN UPSTAIRS

"Ya' talk slang, Man?"

"Yah. I talk slang.

I'm THE MAN—known as the Son of Man.

I made man.

I know your lingo an' I see your swing…

your swaggering moves an' blustering talk.

How 'bout you tryin' My lovin' walk an'

My kindly talk?

As you learn My talk an' My walk,

you'll strut My walk and rock with My

talk."

"Ya dig, man?"

THE DOOR

What 'cha gonna' do, huh?
What 'cha gonna' do?
When the world goes crazy, what 'cha
gonna' do?

Ya gonna' trust My Word or toss it to the
side?
Ya gonna' walk with Me or shut Me
outside?
The choice is yours. It's always yours…
Shut out 'da light or open 'da door?

Ya shut out 'da light, it's dark inside.
Ya open 'da door, it's light inside.
'Da choice is yours. It's always yours…
Shut out 'da light or open 'da door.

*"In him was life, and that life was the light of all mankind.
The light shines in the darkness, and the darkness has not overcome it."*

John 1:4-5 NIV

THE AUTO-MACHINE

You think you have a mean, clean auto-
machine?
Bring Me not only…
the shiny hood and the souped-up engine,
the flashy chrome wheels and the tires that
squeal…
bring Me also…
the leaky seal,
and the creaky seat,
the weak alternator
and the dirty radiator,
the scratch on the dash
and the dent in the door.

With My eye in the sky, I've had you spied.
Hitch a ride with Me. We'll ride high and
wide, mean and clean
in My heavenly powered auto-machine.

INTERCHANGES OF A
REVEALING KIND

"Here, let me hold the door for you."

"That's okay. You don't have to do that."

"When I was at the store, I picked up some fruit and chocolate for you."

"Oh, you shouldn't have done that."

"I bought a rotisserie chicken for us to share."

"Okay. How much do I owe you?"

"I'm paying for your ticket today."

"No! I don't want you to do that."

"Let Me heal your heart."

"No. That's alright. I'll be fine."

Pause. Remember. Go back.

Return to the child still residing within.

Answer again.

"I have a gift of love and acceptance for you. You *are* worthy. Let Me heal your heart."

"Oh, thank you, Daddy! Thank you. I accept Your offer. I receive Your gift. Please heal my heart. I release it into Your hands. Fix it, Father. Fix it."

Fixed.

"Here, let me hold the door for you."

"Well, thank you, sir. That is very kind of you."

"When I was at the store, I picked up some fruit and chocolate for you."

"Wow. My two most favorite foods. Thank you. I will really enjoy snacking on them."

“I bought a rotisserie chicken for us to share.”

“Wonderful. And I have fresh salad. Let’s put them together for a special meal.”

“I’m paying for your ticket today.”

“How gracious of you. I feel so honored you would do that for me.”

And all is well with my soul.

THE TWO BUILDERS

"What good does it do for you to say that I am your Lord and Master if what I teach you is not put into practice? Let me describe the one who truly follows me and does what I say... and the one who has heard and does not obey."
Luke 6:46-49 TPT

The obedient…

Seated in high places.

At rest.

A house on the Rock

Balanced securely

Solid foundation.

The storm, the wind, the rain…

And the house stood

For great was the strength of it.

***

The disobedient…

Seated in self-effort

At high energy.

A house of cards

Balanced precariously

No foundation.

The storm, the wind, the rain…

And the house fell

And great was the fall of it.

"Which of these two builders will you be?"

Luke 6:46-49 TPT

MISSING

Missing in action…
  where have you been?
Souls are dying for lack of men…
  men who with compassion are filled
  and use the Living Word with skill—
  men who are moved with the love of God
  to speak of Jesus who this earth once trod—
  men whose tears flow freely down,
  crying, "Lord, have mercy on this ol'
town!"—
  men whose prayers rise freely upward,
  not using Your Name as a mere cuss
word—
  men consumed with the glory of God
  spreading His fire on this dry, dry sod.

Missing in action…
  Where have you been?

THE NEW CREATION

With an authoritative stance, He surveyed
the scene…
 the farmhouse bedroom of the past,
dwarfed by bare elm trees outside the locked
down windows,
 dust from the wearisome trip of life,
 the musty air of memories rehearsed again
and again,
 narrow spaces behind self-erected walls of
protection,
 broken down chairs of betrayed trusts…
 a heart in disarray.
"Oh, these hang-ups of the past will never
do. They're all excess baggage."
Ignoring my protests, He finishes His
assessment.

Giving me a knowing glance, He beckons
me to a veiled opening in the wall of my
heart and then disappears.

***

That passageway pulsates with serene colors
of blended hues.
A sense of peace and calm reaches out to
draw me in.
Intrigued, I again take a chance on life.
Slipping into freedom, I leave the crimping
captivity of my old heart; with joy I enter
the unlimited space of my spirit—the new
creation.

> *"Therefore, if anyone is in Christ, the new*
> *creation has come: The old has gone, the*
> *new is here!"*
> *II Cor. 5:17 NIV*

VICTORY

*"But thanks be to God! He gives us the
victory through our Lord Jesus Christ."*
I Cor. 15:57 NIV

IT IS FINISHED

The proclamation reverberates through the

hallways of heaven

and the corridors of time—

forever echoing the vibrations of victory,

the loosing of the bound,

the freedom of the captives and

the shouts of joy.

Creating…

confusion in the ranks of evil,

havoc in the camp of the enemy and

terror within the tormentors.

"It is finished."

The words resound in the hearts of men.

They draw a line in the sands of time.

"Who is for Me and who is against Me?"

Decide.

The issue within must be settled.

The Light comes blindingly to the forefront.

No time remaining.

It is either Truth in total surrender or

darkness in total rebellion.

Which one will you choose?

THE KEEPER OF THE KEYS

I AM the keeper of the keys.

No one shall rip them from My hand.

None who come against Me shall stand.

I AM the keeper of all the earth.

Without Me there is no mirth.

"Destroyer, give Me a wide berth."

I AM the keeper of life and death,

The only One who enables breath.

Love, to My Bride, I profess.

I AM the keeper of the keys.

I open doors for you to seize

what Satan has stolen—just believe.

THE REMNANT

There's a stirring in the sky.

Feel it? Hear it, coming nigh?

'Tis the hosts of heaven in battle array

Breaking through the clouds of gray.

It is for such a time as this

They've waited in the heavenly mist.

But now released they are

To battle near and far.

They carry the war cry of the coming King;

Their voices with true victory ring.

"Repent, for the time in now at hand

To bring together the remnant band."

The remnant reflects the glory of God,

Purified under the Shepherd's rod.

No earthly fear in them abides;

Perfect love has cast it aside.

The fear of the Lord they carry inside;
    The name of Christ they will not hide.
In the Redeemer their life is hid
    No more of the enemy of which to be rid.

So the remnant goes forth with the heavenly
host;
    Only in the Lord do they make their boast.
"Come to the King; receive His love,
    Then you'll be fit for heaven above."

A NEW SOUND

There's a new sound coming to this land.
It's the sound of My people taking a stand.
Though the enemy has long barred the gates,
My remnant will no longer yield and wait.

My body will arise with Me as their Head.
To redeem them all, I once bled.
My people will take the land by storm
And evil no longer will be the norm.

My glory will shine from deep within
For their hearts will be pure—cleansed from
sin.
My kingdom's reign will begin right now
And enemy tyrants to Me will bow.

A CALL TO BATTLE

Sound the warning!

Sound the alarm!

The enemy is coming to do you harm.

Take your stand,

Lift your hand;

Gather all your Christian band.

Together we will make our stand.

The time is ripe—

There's anger and strife.

Bend your knee,

Become all you can be.

For this you are here…

The enemy plans to sear.

Be strong and brave…

Like a warrior behave.

I am with you

To cover and keep you.

Take My hand

And make your stand!

THE STORM

The storm clouds are gathering…
All demons are chattering.
The darkness rests heavy;
Let God's people be ready.

The air hangs hot with sweat
From the enemies' threats.
The battle is joined;
Troops are deployed.

The forces of darkness gather in glee,
Approaching those on bended knee.
But, all ablaze the King appears.
Assailants now must flee in fear.

Lightning flashes from east to west,
Leaving the foe not a second of rest.
For the King of Light goes forth to fight

In the cause of truth and for the sake of
right.

THE TIME IS NOW

The drumbeat of heaven, beating on the
Earth:
"The time is now.
Bend and bow!"

The indignation of heaven, resounding on
the Earth:
"Bow in fear.
The King is near."

The soundboard of heaven, reverberating in
the Earth:
"Near at hand
The Judge does stand."

The gates of heaven shut, thundering on the
Earth:
"Stand and implore,

But closed is the door."

"He will open doors that no one can shut,

and he will shut doors that no one can

open."

Isaiah 22:22b TPT

—A TRILOGY—

THE QUESTION

I awake.

Instantly on high spiritual alert, my entire

being picks up on a heavenly urgency.

An atmospheric weight crushes down on my

chest, pinning me to the bed.

I gasp for air.

Crashing cymbals ring in my ears.

The clanging of swords reverberates in

every molecule of my flesh.

A denseness of conflict drops from the sky,

tensing my shoulders.

I forget to breathe.

A darkness drips upon the earth.

A cry rips through lips tightened with fright.

What is to happen?

When forces of fear press forward, how will

peace prevail?

THE CRYING OUT

Weeping, I fall to my knees, crying out,
"What am I to do, Lord?
I'm bruised and broken, overwhelmed by it
all.
Fear has so paralyzed me that I can do
nothing.
Stuck in a maze of indecision, I know not
which way to turn, or which way is out.
Help me!"

Psalm 119:10 TPT

THE ANSWER

Quietness
A holy hush.

Serene peace begins invading the darkness
of fear,
followed by a strong surge of electrical
energy coursing through my body.
The skin on my arms tightens, raising up
goose bumps.

My heart responds in kind, pushing open its
ear gates, as if to listen.
I wait.
A still, small whisper.
"Have I not told you? Be not afraid. I am
with you. I will lead you.
My Word is a lamp unto your feet and a
light unto your path.
I hold you by your right hand. Nothing will
harm you.
Now, arise. Stand. Trust Me.
I will stay close to you and show you the
way you should go.

Nothing will ever be able to separate you

from My love.

Rest and be at peace."

Jer. 1:17, 19 NLT   Ps. 119:105 TPT   Ps. 32:8 TPT   Rom. 8:39 NIV

—A TRILOGY—

THE DEFEAT OF FEAR

Darkness reigns, but light pierces the sky—

beginning in the east and streaking to the

west.

Just so, Fear is defeated, falling in a flash.

The first shall be last and the last shall be

first.

Behold, so sudden, so quick, the end shall

come…a turning.

The downtrodden uplifted—the exalted

brought low

at the coming of the awesome day of the

Lord.

Lift up your heads. Your King draws nigh…

for all eternity,

ruling and reigning on high.

THE FALL OF FEAR

The atmosphere, charged with electricity.

A crackling in the air.

No time to huddle.

No time to stay.

Rise up and go.

Run, with head bowed low.

Seek shelter from the rain and cold before

the night grows old.

Your reign has ended, Fear.

You stumble and fall.

Your kingdom crashes.

The reign of peace is here.

THE DEATH OF FEAR

The Prince of Peace tightens the noose

'round Fear's neck.

See.

It struggles for air.

It twitches and turns, but it cannot be loosed.

It relaxes its grip.

It draws it last breath.

It's over. It's done.

The victims now become the victors, and

peace is loosed upon the earth.

A SHIFT

There's a new sound a-takin' hold on this
earth.
Ya' can feel the risin' rhythm and sense the
pulsin' beat
As you are a-snappin' your fingers and a-
tappin' your feet.

There's a new move in the kingdom,
A shift in the air.
Fears are a-fly'n, terror everywhere.

The enemy's a-movin' out-a this land.
Grab a hold a-the King; grip tightly to His
hand;
He will soon lead y'all to His Promised
Land.

TRIUMPH

Out of the dark and out of the deep
   Leviathan rises up from his sleep.
His strength is great, and fierce is he,
   But his time on earth short will be.

Take note of his presence to be on guard;
   But know that God's Fire melts his might
like lard.
The glory of Christ is greater by far, and
   To the Serpent, heaven's gates will be
barred.

You are in Christ and Christ is in you;
   The enemies fall and soon will be few.
Take heart and boldly step out of the pack
   To lead with Christ the frontal attack.

Leviathan falls before the Triumphant Few

As they stand and leave the worn, church
pews…
Out into the streets, their heads held high
    As the banner of Christ in triumph they
fly!

TOGETHER

It's just Him and me for all the world to
see…

   No mask, no pretense, just together, as we
were always meant to be.
All excuses dropped; all mistakes forgot.

   In no more traps to be caught, for my
freedom has been bought.

It's time to move on with Him; in His
shelter I will flee.

   No more pushing, pulling; in Him I am set
free.

Why did I run and struggle so long? My
strength was all but gone.

   With Him, I now have the might for which
I've longed.

Forward with Him I quickly will move;
together there's so much yet to do,
    For the world lies spread before us, and
the victory is ours to pursue.

THE MAN

There once was a man who walked this
earth.
In humility He was birthed.
No pride, no royal robes,
As a babe, in strips of cloth He was clothed.

A perfect man, no spot on Him.
No blemish, mark or sin.
Nothing of the enemy in Him.
His goal, to redeem all those unloved,
To be the one and only sacrifice of love…
The walk, the cross, the stripping, the
shame.
"Why, why, why?" you cry.
"For you, for you, I died."

Now, in royal robes, He rules and reigns in
heaven above.

From His pierced side had come forth the
one He loved…
His Bride, now seated near Him, right by
His side.
Earthly affairs laid aside,
Eternal issues to now decide.
*"And God raised us up with Christ and
seated us with him in the heavenly realms in
Christ Jesus."*
Eph. 2:6 NIV

GOOD FRIDAY

All alone on earth's damp, dark sod,
there trod One called the Son of God.
The sin, depravity and opposition were
fierce.
It seemed no light could ever pierce.
But this light was carried within the Man
born to this earth in His Father's plan.
He's the Light of Life in the hearts of men
who now can be delivered from what might
have been.
"For it is the God who said, 'Let light shine
out of darkness,'
who has shone in our hearts to give the light
of the knowledge
of the glory of God in the face of Christ."
II Cor. 4:6 RSV

IT IS FINISHED

"So when Jesus had received the sour wine,
He said, "It is finished!" And bowing His
head, He gave up His spirit."
John19:30 NKJ

Up, up and away, into eternity so deep…
The Divine Entity to seek.
Love is His name—
Salvation to be gained.

"It is finished."
The cry of the cross! It echoes into the
corridor of time
Splitting it in two.

BC   AD

JESUS

His blood dripped for me, for you.
Then…

Up from the depths of the NetherRealm

He leapt.

Death's grip was split in two

And the King slipped from the tomb.

"He is no longer here. He is risen!"

He is risen indeed!

"He is not here; for he has risen, as he said.

Come, see the place where he lay."

Matt.28:6 RSV

JOY

Joy~~the music of heaven restoring the heartbeat of hope.

REDISCOVERING JOY

It leaps off the page; it slides off the brush.

It laughs like a child; it smiles in the dark.

It lifts hands to praise and hearts to sing.

It strengthens weak knees to stand.

It settles into peace.

It joins His life.

HE is where the joy is.

"Gaze upon him, join your life with his, and

joy will come."

Ps. 34:5 TPT

JOY

Spiraling upward in a column of pure light

bursting forth in a myriad of colors

falling in sparkles of delight

A HANDFUL OF JOY

"God called the light Day, and the darkness
he called Night."
Gen. 1:5a RSV

When I moved on the face of the deep,
  I did not slumber, nor did I sleep;
I grabbed hold of light and with a handful of
joy
  I released it and spread it like an eager,
young boy.

The light sprang forth and there came to be
Day;
"There was Day, and there was Night," I did
say.

I was so happy, so filled with joy,

Like a small, young boy with a brand-new
toy,
For the light was a part of My very own Self
   To be seen, to be shared—not put on a
shelf.

My love is the same—to be seen, to be
shared.
   It is Me…beautiful, bountiful, surely not
rare.
Take care to release it with a handful of joy
   As you bound through this world as My
own loved boy.

LIFE

Pulsating patterns…

Color

Light

Movement

Music

Joy

An interplay of life on the threshold of

eternity.

Reach out.

Touch it.

IMAGINE

Oh, for balloons to fill a room—

to fill a room with color and light,

to fill a heart with joy and delight…

dancing up and above

lifting the spirit

lifting the mind

from the mundane and sane

into the realm of

imagination—

floating

reaching

stretching

twirling

whirling

daring to believe that I am free

to just be me!

HAVE FUN

The rhythm of life flows out through the night.
Boom baba, boom baba…boom ba!
You'll want to catch that rhythm and feel that
beat.
It will pulsate all the way down to your feet.

It will then rise up from the boards of the floor.
It will vibrate throughout your entire core.
It will pull on your spirit, up and out
To laugh, to sing, to shake and shout.

Rise on up…. come on out. Come for the More.
Be restored.

Boom baba, boom baba…boom ba!
Boom baba, boom baba…boom ba!

COLOR ME BEAUTIFUL

Come and dine with Me.

   Let us partake of the choice wine of My
love.

Sniff the scent of faithfulness.

   Reflect on the hue of gentleness.

Savor the flavors of joy…

   A touch of kindness,

   A taste of goodness,

   A hint of peace,

   A trace of patience.

The wine is called *Color Me Beautiful*.

AN ARRANGEMENT

The creative forever-dance began before the

world began,

before the ages came into being…

undulating movements of DNA,

swirling colors,

exalting angels,

dancing stars,

twirling earth…

an arrangement written in heaven.

THE TREASURE

There's a fancy, yellow house high upon a
hill.
  Inside, all is exceedingly still.
Young and old have deserted this house,
  Even the little, itty-bitty mouse.

All went off in search of treasure,
  Following their own good pleasure.
They did not know that in their home
  Lay a precious gold-jeweled comb.

One day a maiden fair chanced to browse
  Within that fancy, yellow house.
Finding that costly gold-jeweled comb,
  She turned that house into a home.

For she sold that valued golden comb

And with wayward, lonely souls filled the
home.
Their joy, love and laughter without
measure
    Became the house's greatest treasure.

So that huge yellow house high upon a hill
    No longer sits so very, very still.
It gently sounds its lovely trill
    Of love, friendship and good will.

THE CHRISTMAS BELLS

You hear them…tinkling in the knell.

They've a story to tell.

Listen…they're heaven's bells.

They ring out sweet and clear.

"Come near; be of good cheer.

The Christ child now is here."

They sound the call for one and all.

(The shepherds will recall.)

Oh come and hear.

The hosts are near.

The KING is here!

REST

Rest~~being cradled in the arms of Jesus.

THE DWELLING PLACE

A dwelling place exists within the Godhead
of oneness, stillness, completeness…
A place of only perfect peace, love and
unity.

Thus it was before time began, and thus it
will be again…
no beginning,
no end…
BEING…
at rest,
at peace,
at one with Him…
lost in the vastness of Him.

***

This is your place of refuge and rest
where you step off the spinning wheel of
time,

going round and round and round and

step on to the gliding wheel of eternity,

moving only forward and onward in peace.

THE TENT

"Let's make a tent!

Let's play," the children say.

Why? Why is that what the children say?

Why the desire to be in a tent,

To play and rest in a tent?

The tent of meeting!

That is why!

It is the universal longing of the heart to

meet with the King,

To be with the King, to rest with the King.

Ex. 33:7-11 RSV

BREAK OUT

There's a space in time wanting to be
prioritized…
purposes to percolate,
incidents to investigate,
lies to penetrate,
strongholds to infiltrate,
tones to modulate,
hearts to saturate.
Time's racing, pacing, and a-wasting.

STOP!
Drop down.
Be still.
Smoothly, with grace and ease,
Strongly, with vigor and vim,
examine what lies within, where time
ceases, and life begins to be…

the resting place, the source, the root of new beginnings.

"Then, by constantly using your faith, the life of Christ will be released deep inside you, and the resting place of his love will become the very source and root of your life."
Eph. 3:17 TPT

THE JIGSAW PUZZLE PIECE

"Where do I fit, Lord?
I've tried to find my place, but I don't fit
anywhere.
Others have picked me up and tried me here,
there and everywhere."

"Does she fit here? No, I guess not. Put her
to the side till we find the right spot."
Days, weeks and months pass.
"Where's that piece I was looking for? Oh, I
see her. She fell under the table.
Got stepped on too, right under my shoe.
Okay. It looks like she should go right here.
But no matter how I twist or turn her,
she just doesn't quite fit…must be a misfit."
***

However, the Great On-Looker in the sky
sees the whole picture from above.

With tenderness and love, He singles me
out, picks me up and dusts me off.
With the ease of a Master's hand, He fits me
smoothly into His plan.
"Here is where she fits. Just where I need
her."
And the puzzle is complete.

"This is where I fit."

THE WAY TO GO

When you lose your way, go back to what
you know. Let nature show you the way to
go…

the red-railed bridge beckoning you to
pray on its sunbaked planks in the midst of
the day,

Japanese lilac blossoms scenting the air
while cottonwood "fluff" decorates your
hair,

the flutter of a breeze through slender
willow trees,

the everchanging scenes of the clouds
shouting aloud, "We see the way."

a motionless bunny without even a blink—
What does he think?

old croaking bullfrogs on water-soaked
logs,

the twirping of crickets at the close of the
day, safe from harm coming their way…
all finding joy throughout their day.
There is peace in this hidden garden of life,
no strife.
Fireflies light up the night with their magical
glow.
There's a sweet sense of being alone, yet,
known.
So, when you lose your way, go back to
what you know.

THE RETURN

I used to sit in the sun with You. It was my
favorite thing to do.
But then, so sad to say, I lost my way.
Here to go. There to go. No more fun in the
snow.
No more frolicking or sun. Only run, run,
run.
My feet grew weary. My heart grew weak.
Duty and fear routed from me the freedom
to just be me.
Now, that truth I clearly see, and I return to
what life was meant to be.
I go back to where together we had begun…
You and me sitting in the sun. And with You
only, now, I run.
"Return to me."
Mal. 3:7 NIV

THE SEARCH

I searched for You in the night
When You seemed so out of sight.
My heart longed for Your touch
When my day had ceased from rush.

Your Word I opened in the night
And in the depths found Your light.
Resurrection life arose within
As You forgave me all my sin.

Now my soul takes its rest;
In You it knows it's blessed.
Sweet sleep comes at last
As in Your arms You hold me fast.
"In peace I will lie down and sleep, for you
alone, LORD, make me dwell in safety."
Ps. 4:8 NIV

THE DUSK OF LIFE

Diffused sparkles of light shimmer on the lake of our memories.

The completed days of our lives now come to life on the palette of the Master Artist. Not perfect days at the time…

But now, peering through the maze of the past, we rest in a new perspective. We notice God's love, etched on the sharp corners of the canvas, softening the harsh edges.

We appreciate the bend in the river's flow. There, the slowed pace eased us into rest. We recognize how the strength of the Almighty undergirded us when we were weak, how His grace muted the dark colors of anger into the soft shades of forgiveness,

and how His mercy picked us up when we
had fallen.

We perceive His perfect love reflected
over the expanse of our lives.
We acknowledge He has done all things
well.

He has blended the colors of our lives and
produced a masterpiece for the dawn of a
bright new day.

THE DOVE

A dove, the bird of love, dropped by to see

me one day.

He landed but two feet away.

My hand paused in mid-air—

I looked at him;

he looked at me.

It was a holy moment, you see.

So brief, so fleeting, so rare.

Time stopped—our eyes met and stared.

So unexpected…this dove of rest.

A reminder of…my Heavenly Guest.

THE STILLNESS

There's a stillness in time coming down

from above,

coming only from the Father of Love.

Be still...pause…listen and learn

the depths of the mysterious of the glory of

God

as on earth the Son, with the Dove, did trod.

Together they wove a maze of love

leading the sons of men to the Father above.

REVELATION

"*I pray that the Father of glory, the God of our Lord Jesus Christ, would impart to you the riches of the Spirit of wisdom and the Spirit of revelation to know him through your deepening intimacy with him.*"
Eph. 1:17 TPT

THE REVELATION

Who am I?

What is my purpose?

The silence is pregnant with life.

The fullness of revelation…

breaking waters

dilating reality

pushing through darkness

laboring from head to heart

bursting into the light of understanding

delivering a realization.

I am a living being created in the image of

God Almighty.

I am my Father's daughter,

walking in His light,

carrying His anointing,

reflecting His glory.

A SIGN

Dark blue clouds laced with icy silver hang

heavy in the sky…

A sign…new revelation is nigh.

Be alert. Be aware.

Eyes to see; ears to hear

Insight and wisdom are drawing near.

THE FIRST ENCOUNTER

A slender figure of light rises from the dew
of the garden—a female figure—
with long flowing hair falling in waves over
her delicate shoulders.
Vibrant and healthy, her inquisitive eyes
exude life with every inquiring look.
She stands, untainted, pure and innocent,
silhouetted in the warm, morning sunshine.
Her eyes widen, a golden light from within
shining with wonder and anticipation.
As Father leads her deeper into the garden,
her heart pulsates, in search mode.
She knows not for what or whom—only that
she will be complete when her search ends.
A longing deep within her yearns to be
matched.
Driven forward with growing excitement,
her pace quickens.

The air is moist on her tender skin.

Every cell in her body tingles with
anticipation.

Rounding a bend in the grassy pathway, she
catches sight of another shining figure,
taller and more muscular than she.

For the very first time in the history of the
ages, she gazes at her counterpart.

He stands awaiting her.

Adam.

Genesis 1:22 RSV

DO THE MATH

The final equation lies before you.

The time of the end has come.
You calculate, life plus Christ must be the
sum.
But is it?
To the Mathematician of heaven, your
figures submit.

He was present with you before your first
breath.
"Come forth and live," He had said.
Thus, your life began,
along with His multiplication plan.

Joy was multiplied, a time and many times
again.

The probability of pain was subtracted, and
grief was divided.
Betrayal was transposed to the
circumference and hurts to the perimeter.
Loneliness was cancelled out—long-time
friends were carried over.

You added God as your true, guiding light.
This angled the Son on your path to be more
and more bright.
Trust and reliance were factored into each
day
as the Spirit of Love held steady sway.

In the last analysis, the end will now the
beginning become,
and life will go on to equal more than a sum.
It will be the product of a time lived well in
the realm down here
and multiplied in the Kingdom that is fast
drawing near.

APPEARANCES

We live in an imperfect world,
but…
we are "perfect" people
living "perfect" lives
holding "perfect" jobs
having "perfect" families…
forgetting
The One Perfect Man.

MOMENTUM

A rocky mountain slope,

glittering diamonds of stone shimmering

in the sun…

you see the scope of what beckons

below…

an ever so slight nudge of the Spirit

and with increasing speed you are ushered

down the

slope into the luminous depths of the

riches and wisdom and knowledge of God.

"O the depths of the riches and wisdom and

knowledge of God."

Rom.11:33a NIV

GLIMPSES OF THE ETERNAL REALM

"As we look not to the things that are seen but to the things that are unseen. For the things that are seen are transient, but the things that are unseen are eternal."

II Cor. 4:18 ESV

A GLIMPSE

"Come up here," the trumpet voice spoke.
In eager surrender we rise, slipping earth's
bounds, entering with ease through the
heavenly portal Himself, The Door.
Awe-filled fear and wonder overtake us as
we find ourselves ushered into the throne
room of the King—the High King, exalted
Ruler of heaven and earth…the Source of all
revelation knowledge, glory and power.
Living colors swirl 'round about us, rising
from the crystal sea of glass. The
atmosphere is supercharged with thunder,
lightning and voices, but the emerald green
rainbow encircling the throne reflects only
grace and mercy. Absorbing the pure
essence of His holiness, we, however, are
oblivious to everything except His presence.
The angels sing, "Holy, holy."

The anthem rings, "Holy, holy is the Lamb

who was slain."

And then, just as easily as we had come, we

slip away from that spirit realm. Dropping

back into the bonds of earth, we bow in

tender surrender on the floor.

"Holy, holy, holy is the Lamb."

As it is in heaven, so shall it be on earth.

Rev. 4 RSV

THE JOINING

With delicate grace the dreaming ballerina

spins and swirls through the ethereal realm.

Loosed from the confines of the flesh, her

spirit is exquisitely adorned; sparkling

strands of delicate gossamer are woven into

her every movement amid the celestial

atmosphere.

The light, easy flow through time and space

fills her with buoyant delight.

Gliding in effortless grace, she daintily

bounces on the tips of her toes.

Then, in one lithe leap,

she reaches for the beckoning stars and the

One who breathed them into existence.

Her expectant spirit rises in inexpressible

joy to meet the approaching Bridegroom.

There, in the ethereal realm, she joins the

Lover of her soul, and they merge into one
spirit.
*"But he who is joined to the Lord becomes
one spirit with him."*
I Cor. 6:17 ESV

EYES THAT BEHOLD

"Have you entered the storehouses of the

snow..."

Job 38:22a RSV

From the storehouses of heaven, You release
the snow.

It twirls and swirls; the wind has it in tow.
It cannot be captured;
It only enraptures
Eyes that behold and hearts that believe.

Eyes that behold above and beyond the
natural—

deep into the purity of the heart set apart:
the delicate settling of peace,
the glistening tears of joy,
the powdery touch of gentleness,
the feathery cushion of kindness,
the pristine beauty of faithfulness and

the crystalline structure of self-control…

all igniting the warmth of love in a cold,

cold world.

A HOLY MOMENT

Swinging open…

A door in the natural,

A portal into the supernatural—

A touching of heaven and earth.

In the stillness, a Presence.

In the silence,

One Who speaks louder than words.

A merging

A union

The Creator

With

The created one…

WHOLENESS

COMPLETENESS.

A CHANGING OF THE GUARD

The womb of night gently slips into morn.

Twinkling stars fade from sight.

Daylight filters through the colors of dawn

while

a horizon of light kisses the moon

goodnight.

Sleepers stir from dreams as fingers of

imaginings grab hold of reality,

and the guard of the night slips away into

obscurity.

A CHRISTMAS MIRACLE

The night air spread its wings to rise high in
the sky.
The stars sparkled and strained to be the first
to see.
The moon gleamed its soft golden glow,
giving glance after glance at the globe
below.

***

A sigh…a cry…a breath…held long and
hard—giving birth to life,
The very…God of Life!
*"In him was life, and the life was the light of
men."*
John 1:1 RSV

THE STARS

Stars, breathed into existence, speaking a
language of their very own,
draw me onward, heavenward, homeward.
Their celestial canopy defuses light into the
night,
truth into darkness,
direction to the lost
and guidance to the wise.
Their twinkling network sparks
imaginations,
extends hope,
soothes sorrow
and stirs up wonder.

*"By the word of the LORD the heavens were
made,
their starry host by the breath of his mouth."*
Psalm 33:6 NIV

the continuum

"For I received from the Lord what I also passed on to you: The Lord Jesus, on the night he was betrayed, took bread, and when he had given thanks, he broke it and said, 'This is my body, which is for you; do this in remembrance of me.' In the same way, after supper he took the cup, saying, 'This cup is the new covenant in my blood; do this, whenever you drink it, in remembrance of me.'"

I Cor. 11:23-25 NIV

…intertwined
   intermingled
   in the taking of the Bread and the Wine,
   the essence of the Spirit above and mine
below…
   together we cross the bridge of the soul,

the intersection of time and eternity,

walking on the water of life,

partaking of that which was bought at

such great sacrifice…

Written while my mother, Erna, was in the nursing home, shortly before her return to her heavenly Father.

THE DISTILLATION

Frail

    Slow

        Weak

            Fragile in body.

But…

    Full

        Vibrant

            Luxurious

                Blossoming

in spirit…

distilled into the pure essence of the
aroma of God. Self, melted into nothingness
with only love remaining.

FIRE

"My love for you has my heart on fire!"

Ps. 69:9 TPT

PRAYERS OF FIRE
(A TRILOGY)

BURNING

Let me burn for You…

A torch for all to see.

Let me burn for You…

In truth and purity.

Kindle the fire;

Let the flame rise higher.

Set it ablaze with love for You.

MY DESIRE

Renewed to burn within Your heart so

true…

Reawaken my desire for only You.

Rekindle Your fire in me.

Reactivate, refresh,

Revitalize.

STRIKE MY HEART

Strike my heart to light Your match of

purity.

Your holy flame burning away all impurity.

Let it be Your hot, white flame

Consuming all my guilt and shame

Until I stand before You, pure, my heart

reclaimed.

*"But John made it clear by telling them,
'There is one coming who is mightier than I.
He is supreme. In fact, I'm not worthy of
even being his slave. I can only baptize you
in this river, but he will baptize you into the
Spirit of holiness and into his raging fire.'"*
Luke 3:16 TPT

HEAR THE CALL

Oh, the sanctuary is so cold,

the fire so low…

old rituals,

old formulas,

old traditions.

Away with the old.

See that cracked wineskin, covered with

callous mold? It lies there

in the ashes of a fire gone cold.

Behold! A new arises…a supple wineskin

to carry the fiery, fresh wine from

the blazing heart of God.

Take the ignited coals from the altar of His

heart.

Kindle within the formative wineskin, a

flaming fire—

one that will never be extinguished,

will never grow cold,
and never grow old.

Release the fiery wine to flow into the
nations,
to bring the peoples into the light of His
glory.

This is the call of the hour. This is for
now.

Come forth, O fire of God!
Have Your way.
Have Your say.
For You are Yahweh.

THE FIRE

At first one thinks it's only a dream
   That fire could burn so deep and clean.
Who knew the King of Fire would come so
soon
   To cleanse my hidden, inner rooms?

As He enters my heart with eyes aflame,
   I know I'll never again be the same.
The chaff and the stubble are set ablaze;
   The serpent's presence He now does raze.

In the embers and ashes lay the dead
snakeskin
   Robbed of life, power and sin.
The path ahead will lead to life
   Lived for the Master with no more strife.

Now my heart burns clean and pure;

My love for the King is deep and sure.

The flame within burns hot and blue

Forever to keep me faithful and true.

Rev. 1:12-16 NIV

THE REMNANT

The edifice rose before me, awe-inspiring in
both size and form,
with vaulted ceilings and marbled floors
adorned…
raised, intended and erected for God's glory.
Now, His image lies marred and scarred, all
but unrecognizable,
relegated, neglected and ignored behind
ornate, locked doors.
In its place a new form has arisen—the spirit
of religion,
hidden, masked and holding fast…
institutionalized but unrecognized,
structured and polished,
domesticated but void of life,
all living remnants discarded…

***

a remnant here and a remnant there,

remnants carrying smoldering embers

everywhere.

Spirit breath joins the Living Word…here a

touch and there a touch…

a hovering, a brooding, an intermingling, a

weaving, a releasing…

Ignition!

Spontaneous combustion everywhere.

Fire in the ranks!

The remnant—all breathing out anew His

fiery power and life,

In place for such a time as this.

"Then all at once a pillar of fire appeared

before their eyes. It separated into tongues

of fire that engulfed each one of them."

Acts 2:3 TPT

—A TRILOGY—

THE RING

Raindrops of fire from the eyes of the

King…

reflected in them, the image of the ring…

the new covenant ring, given us by the King.

THE FLAME

The blue flame of love from above

Now burns in the hearts of men below.

It longs…it yearns…it burns

To reach all peoples high and low,

Leaning in to love the One who brings no

woe.

THE RAIN

Burn, burn within me; burn up the dross
Till it be nothing but loss.
Burn, burn within me
Till there is nothing lame…only gain.
Burn, burn within me
Till I'm aflame with the rain…the Latter
Rain of the Kingdom of God.

RESURRECTION POWER

*"...and the earth quaked, and the rocks were
split, and the graves were opened; and the
bodies of the saints who had fallen asleep
were raised..."*
Matt. 27:51b-52 NKJV

The earth shook.

Graves opened.

The dead rose.

***

Hell shook.

Foundations split.

Walls crumbled; gates tumbled.

Blinding light burst upon the scene; fire

disrupted fiendish glee.

Weapons burned; faces melted.

Piercing pain through demon toes; groans

deep and low.

Lightning crackled in the air.

Darkness shattered; strongholds blasted.

Panic in the camp—disarray, dismay.

Tremors of horror, dread, alarm.

Then, paralyzing shock…no longer One to

mock.

***

Keys snatched.

Victory at last.

"CHRIST IS RISEN."

He is risen indeed.

INTIMACY

"Become intimate with him in whatever you do, and he will lead you wherever you go."

Prov. 3:6 TPT

JESUS

Jesus, Your presence, so heavy, so near, so

dear—

Tenderly wooing

Lovingly embracing

Gently touching

Expectantly hovering

So heavy, so near, so dear.

THE HEALER

Raw, red meat…

   my heart.

Tender to the touch…

   my heart

Lonely, forsaken…

   my heart.

"Oh, who will heal my broken heart?" I cry.

"Jesus, keep me near the cross,

There a precious fountain

Free to all, a healing stream,

Flows from Calvary's mountain."

Fanny Crosby 1869

Jesus!   Jesus!   Jesus!

"The Spirit of the Lord is upon me, because

the Lord has anointed me

To bring good tidings to the afflicted;

He has sent me to bind up the

brokenhearted...to comfort all who mourn."

Is. 61:1-2 ESV

ADRIFT

Adrift in the world

With no anchor to hold

The craft of my life in the dark and the cold.

So lonely—alone—

With no place to go

And no one to hold.

I know not where I'm going,

I see nothing ahead but the Blood

That for me once was shed.

So, Master, come into my vessel

And sail with me.

Then safe I will be on the stormy sea

THE TEST

I recognized Him not.

Kind, He was, yes…just so ordinary.

I hear the angry shouts from down the street.

"Find Him. Get Him!"

Fearful alarm bells ring within me.

"They're looking for You! Go, before they

find you."

And I turn Him out, barefoot, into the cold

with nowhere else to go.

***

Ashamed, I turn inward.

"What have I done? Oh, no! I have betrayed

the King, the One my soul loves."

To the door I run.

Is it too late?

"I'm sorry. Come back. I want to make

room for You."

He stops. He turns to look at me.

"Come back. I will hide You in my heart. I

want You here. With me."

His hair is already damp with the night air,

but a smile gladdens His face.

I run to embrace Him.

I lead Him into the inner sanctuary of my

heart to cherish Him there.

And I am safe!

Song of Songs 3:4; 8:2 TPT

THE TENT OF MEETING

"Come…"

He extends His hand in love.

Rising, I place my hand in His.

With tender anticipation, He leads me to the

"tent of meeting,"

covering me with His presence.

There, in the sweet darkness, my heart

yields to His entreaties

and drinks the wine of His love.

"But let them be glad, those who turn aside

to hide themselves in you.

May they keep shouting for joy forever!

Overshadow them in your presence as they

sing and rejoice."

Ps. 5:11a TPT

YOUR WAY

Guide and direct me through the day.

Show me how to walk Your way.

Have Your say in my day;

Let me shine Your rays.

LOVE

A tender touch,

A loving embrace,

And all is well.

DEPENDENCE

Lord, lead me each step of the way.

Let me lean on You for guidance each day.

Your will I seek as I walk through each

week.

Wrap Your strength 'round my loins as with

You I am joined.

Remain my all in all 'til I hear Your clarion

call.

A PRAYER

Let my words drip with love

for the kingdom above.

No earthly bond I know;

but into Thee I grow

until I'm deeply rooted

And sure-footed

In the love of Christ, my King.

To Thee my praises ring!

QUICKEN ME

"My soul cleaveth unto the dust:
Quicken thou me according to thy word."
Ps. 119:25 KJV

In the dust my soul cleaves.
　　Lord, is there no help for me?
Come and fill me with Thy life
　　Lest I pass away in endless strife.

Let Your breath in me abound;
　　Encircle me round and round.
Quicken me with Thy Word
　　Let it firm in me be heard.

SEPARATED

Separated unto You;

No one else will do.

In Your arms hold me tight…

I am Your garden of delight.

"My lover has gone down into his garden of delight, the place where his spices grow, to feast with those pure in heart. We shall find him there. He is within me—I am his garden of delight. I have him fully and now he fully has me!"

Song of Sg. 6:2-3 TPT

UNITED

You did it all
  You did it all for me.
Loved
  You loved me with Your all
    Submitted in love to Your Father's call.
Forgiven
  You've forgiven all in me
    And now I'm free.
Free
  Submitted in all I do.
    Surrendered and finally free,
  To give my life to You
    Submitted and free to simply…be.
Now
  In all, we move together
    Intermingled, to freely live and move
together.
        United…in totality.

"For in Him we live and move and have our

being."

Acts 17:28 NIV

COME

-*An Open Invitation*-

Come to Me in the night hours;

In My presence fear does cower.

Be strong; be bold

And of My hand take hold.

Together, we will cross the stream of time

And forever then, you'll be Mine.

My heart yearns to touch your face

All edged with white wedding lace.

You are so delicate and fair

With lovely flowing hair.

Come quickly into My soft embrace

And let Me gaze at your sweet face.

I COME

-An Invitation Accepted-
My King, I come; I come. Leave me not.
For Your embrace, this battle have I fought.
Your love hath me sustained,
The ultimate prize to gain.

Your love to me flows like wine,
Your essence, infinitely divine.
I long for You in depths so deep;
My soul, O Lord, safe do keep.

Your breeze o're me so gently blows
To refresh me here below;
It brings to me Your soothing touch…
With You I choose to linger—ne'er again to
rush.

WELCOME HOME

The time has come; the end is near.

Take His hand, my dear.

Walk with Him through gates of pearl

As exultantly the angels whirl

In joy unspeakable above

To welcome home the one who's loved.

(Written in honor of my dear mother)

THE BRIDE

*"Then one of the seven angels who had the
seven bowls full of the last seven plagues
came to me and said, 'Come. I will show you
the beautiful bride, the wife of the Lamb.'
He carried me away in the realm of the
Spirit to the top of a great, high mountain.
There he showed me the holy city,
Jerusalem, descending out of heaven from
God. It was infused with the glory of God,
and its radiance was like a jasper, clear as
crystal."*
Rev. 21:9b-11 TPT

THE BRIDE

Beyond expression

Belief

Comprehension
Eternity…

Exquisite in beauty,
Shimmering in light
Brilliant in purity
Gleaming in richness
Pulsating in love…the Bride.

THE PRESENTATION OF THE BRIDE

"I also saw the holy city, a new Jerusalem, coming down out of heaven from God, prepared as a bride adorned for her husband."
Rev.21:2 NIV

Cleansed in the blood

Perfected in holiness

Flawless in character

Purified in flame

Burnished in fire

Fortified in adversity

Magnificent in strength

Energized with life

Filled with the Spirit

Overflowing with love…the BRIDE

"The Spirit and the bride say, 'Come!'

And let the one who hears say, 'Come!'

Let the one who is thirsty come;

*and let the one who wishes take the free gift of
the water of life.*

He who testifies to these things says,

'Yes, I am coming soon.'

Amen. Come, Lord Jesus.

*The grace of the Lord Jesus be with God's
people.*

Amen."

Rev. 22:17, 20-21 NIV

ABOUT THE AUTHOR

Connie Victoria Volk has always claimed the starry, wide-open country of the Dakotas as home.

After graduating from Northern State College in Aberdeen, SD, she taught English and Spanish in various mid-western schools.

After the death of her husband and mother, she pursued her passion for writing and her family's love of painting.

Connie carries an enthusiasm for life, bringing encouragement and joy into the lives of others.

She is blessed with two wonderful daughters and three grandchildren.

She was one of the first members of the Healing Rooms of the Northern Plains and a Director of the Healing Room Kids.

Also by Connie Victoria Volk

Explore Connie's website at

https://connievolk.com

COPYRIGHT

Copyright © 2024 Connie Victoria Volk

The scriptural references are taken from The Passion Translation (TPT), New International Version (NIV), King James Version (KJV), New King James Version (NKJV), Revised Standard Version (RSV), English Standard Version (ESV), New Living Translation (NLT) or The Message (MSG). Each identifying version is noted with each scriptural passage throughout the book.

ISBN: 9798986495644

Cover design by Solutions Website Design.

Author photo by Andra Marquardt.

ALSO BY CONNIE VICTORIA VOLK:

The Hidden Place

The Hidden Place Study Guide